Peaches
Mangoes
Figs
Citrus
Apples
Peaches

PLANTS WE EAT

Mangoes
Figs
Citrus
Apples
Peaches
Mangoes
Figs
Citrus
Apples
Peaches
Mangoes
Figs
Citrus

Tall and Tasty
Fruit Trees

Meredith Sayles Hughes

Lerner Publications Company/Minneapolis

Check out the author's website at www.foodmuseum.com/hughes

Lerner Publications Company
A Division of Lerner Publishing Group
241 First Avenue North
Minneapolis, MN 55401 U.S.A.

Website address: www.lernerbooks.com

Designer: Steven P. Foley
Editors: Katy Holmgren, Chris Dall
Photo Researcher: Dan Mahoney

LIBRARY OF CONGRESS CATALOGING-IN-PUBLICATION DATA

Hughes, Meredith Sayles.
    Tall and Tasty : Fruit Trees / by Meredith Sayles Hughes.
      p. cm. – (Plants we eat)
    Includes index.
    Summary: Describes the historical origins, uses, and growing requirements of various fruit trees, such as the apple, peach, mango, and fig. Includes recipes.
    ISBN 0–8225–2837–1 (lib. bdg. : alk. paper)
    1. Fruit—Juvenile literature. 2. Cookery (Fruit) Juvenile literature. [1. Fruit.] I. Title. II. Series: Hughes, Meredith Sayles. Plants we eat.
SB357.2.H83 2000
634—dc21   99–18758

Manufactured in the United States of America.
1 2 3 4 5 6 – JR – 05 04 03 02 01 00

The glossary on page 77 gives definitions of words shown in **bold type** in the text.

Contents

Introduction

Plants make all life on our planet possible. They provide the oxygen we breathe and the food we eat. Think about a burger and fries. The meat comes from cattle, which eat plants. The fries are potatoes cooked in oil from soybeans, corn, or sunflowers. The burger bun is a wheat product. Ketchup is a mixture of tomatoes, herbs, and corn syrup or the sugar from sugarcane. How about some onions or pickle relish with your burger?

How Plants Make Food

By snatching sunlight, water, and carbon dioxide from the atmosphere and mixing them together—a complex process called **photosynthesis**—green plants create food energy. The raw food energy is called glucose, a simple form of sugar. From this storehouse of glucose, each plant produces fats, carbohydrates, and proteins—the elements that make up the bulk of the foods humans and animals eat.

Sunlight peeks through the branches of a plant-covered tree in a tropical rain forest, where all the elements exist for photosynthesis to take place.

First we eat, then we do everything else.

—M. F. K. Fisher

Plants offer more than just food. They provide the raw materials for making the clothes you're wearing and the paper in books, magazines, and newspapers. Much of what's in your home comes from plants—the furniture, the wallpaper, and even the glue that holds the paper on the wall. Eons ago plants created the gas and oil we put in our cars, buses, and airplanes. Plants even give us the gum we chew.

On the Move

Although we don't think of plants as beings on the move, they have always been pioneers. From their beginnings as algaelike creatures in the sea to their movement onto dry land about 400 million years ago, plants have colonized new territories. Alone on the barren rock of the earliest earth, plants slowly established an environment so rich with food, shelter, and oxygen that some forms of marine life took up residence on dry land. Helped along by birds who scattered seeds far and wide, plants later sped up their travels, moving to cover most of our planet.

Early in human history, when few people lived on the earth, gathering food was everyone's main activity. Small family groups were nomadic, venturing into areas that offered a source of water, shelter, and foods such as fruits, nuts, seeds, and small game animals. After they had eaten up the region's food sources, the family group moved on to another spot. Only when people noticed that food plants were renewable—that the berry bushes would bear fruit again and that grasses gave forth seeds year after year—did family groups begin to settle in any one area for more than a single season.

Domestication of plants probably began as an accident. Seeds from a wild plant eaten at dinner were tossed onto a trash pile. Later a plant grew there, was eaten, and its seeds were tossed onto the pile. The cycle continued on its own until someone noticed the pattern and repeated it deliberately. Agriculture radically changed human life. From relatively small plots of land, more people could be fed

It's a Fact!

The term *photosynthesis* comes from Greek words meaning "putting together with light." This chemical process, which takes place in a plant's leaves, is part of the natural cycle that balances the earth's store of carbon dioxide and oxygen.

Native Americans were the first peoples to plant crops in the Americas.

over time, and fewer people were required to hunt and gather food. Diets shifted from a broad range of wild foods to a more limited but more consistent menu built around one main crop such as wheat, corn, cassava, rice, or potatoes. With a stable food supply, the world's population increased and communities grew larger. People had more time on their hands, so they turned to refining their skills at making tools and shelter and to developing writing, pottery, and other crafts.

Plants We Eat

This series examines the wide range of plants people around the world have chosen to eat. You will discover where plants came from, how they were first grown, how they traveled from their original homes, and where they have become important and why. Along the way, each book looks at the impact of certain plants on society and discusses the ways in which these food plants are sown, harvested, processed, and sold. You will also discover that some plants are key characters in exciting high-tech stories. And there are plenty of opportunities to test recipes and to dig into other hands-on activities.

The series Plants We Eat divides food plants into a variety of informal categories. Some plants are prized for their seeds, others for their fruits, and some for their underground roots, tubers, or bulbs. Many plants offer leaves or stalks for good eating. Humans convert some plants into oils and others into beverages or flavorings.

In *Tall and Tasty: Fruit Trees*, we'll take a look at fruits that grow on trees. The part of a plant that develops from a flower and contains the plant's seeds is called a fruit. **Pollination** allows the flower to become a fruit. Fruit's role in nature is to ensure that new plants will grow from the old. Many fruits also provide food for people and animals. Fruits include apples, peaches, figs, mangoes, and citrus—the foods that we'll discuss in this book.

You may be surprised to learn that citrus fruits—oranges, lemons, and grapefruit, to name a few—are considered berries. A true berry is a single, enlarged ovary (the part of a flower that becomes a fruit) with many seeds embedded in its flesh. The crisp, tasty apple is a pome—that is, a fruit with a papery core that encloses the seeds. Peaches and mangoes are both drupes, which means that the fruits have a hard pit surrounding a seed. Figs are multiple fruits. They develop from a cluster of flowers borne on the same stem. The soft, tasty part that we eat surrounds many tiny fruits that people usually consider to be seeds.

Fruit trees are perennial plants, which means that they live for several years. Although they can grow in the wild, many of these trees thrive in orderly orchards and groves where workers tend them. They have to be planted in certain regions that provide the right growing conditions. Mangoes flourish in the **tropics.** Apples and peaches live in the **temperate zone.** Figs and citrus fruits do best in **subtropical** regions. A long frost (when the temperature stays below 32 degrees for several days) can prove fatal to these trees.

At harvesttime, careful workers pick the fragile fruit. These fruits are eaten fresh all around the world or turned into a wide range of jams, jellies, drinks, desserts, stews, and breads.

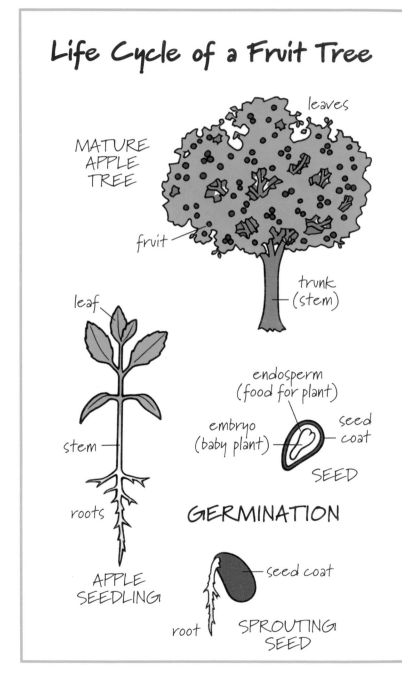

Life Cycle of a Fruit Tree

MATURE APPLE TREE

leaves

fruit

trunk (stem)

leaf

stem

roots

APPLE SEEDLING

endosperm (food for plant)

embryo (baby plant)

seed coat

SEED

GERMINATION

seed coat

root

SPROUTING SEED

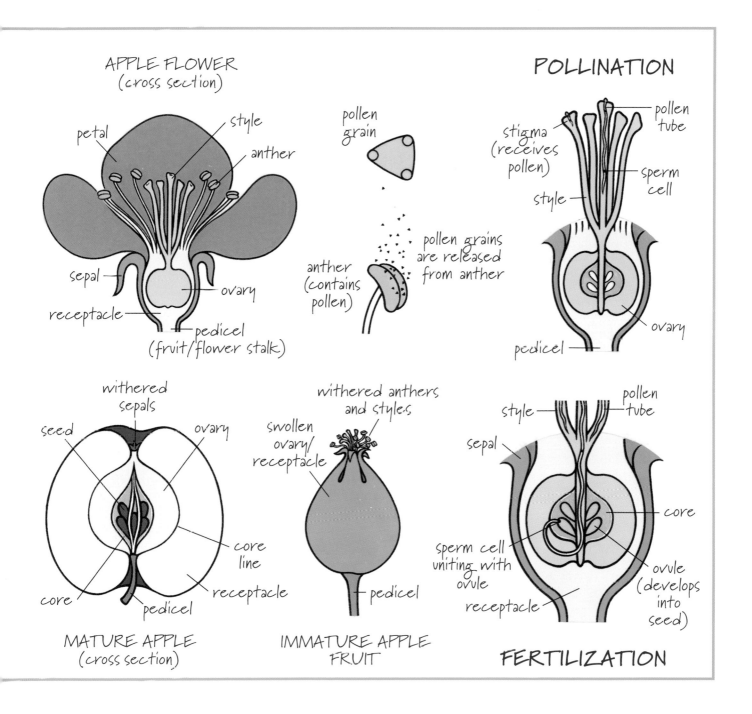

APPLE FLOWER
(cross section)

petal

style

anther

sepal

ovary

receptacle

pedicel
(fruit/flower stalk)

pollen
grain

anther
(contains
pollen)

pollen grains
are released
from anther

POLLINATION

stigma
(receives
pollen)

pollen
tube

sperm
cell

style

ovary

pedicel

MATURE APPLE
(cross section)

withered
sepals

seed

ovary

core
line

core

pedicel

receptacle

IMMATURE APPLE
FRUIT

withered anthers
and styles

swollen
ovary/
receptacle

pedicel

FERTILIZATION

style

pollen
tube

sepal

core

sperm cell
uniting with
ovule

ovule
(develops
into
seed)

receptacle

Apples
[Malus]

The apple is so much a part of world culture that its name evokes both the best and the worst. A "bad apple" is someone who spreads problems—one bad or rotten apple in a barrel of stored apples can spread the rot throughout the barrel. The eye's pupil has been called "apple of the eye," a phrase that also means a special favorite. Ancient legends tell of wars that began over golden apples, and the biblical tree of knowledge is often said to have been the apple tree.

A member of the Rosaceae family (the rose family), the apple tree's blossoms resemble tiny, old-fashioned roses. And there is a hint of the rose in the aroma of sweet varieties of apple. Rosaceae includes pomes such as pears and quinces (an applelike fruit).

The red and yellow Braeburn apple is one of thousands of apple varieties.

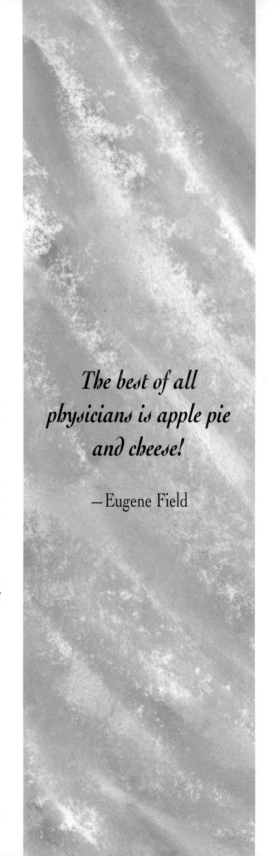

The best of all physicians is apple pie and cheese!

—Eugene Field

Every fruit has an official, scientific Latin name. Apples are so important that the botanical name for the apple genus—*Malus*—originally referred to any big fruit tree. And the modern-day French and Italian words for apple *(pomme* and *pomo)* have their beginnings in the Latin word that means fruit, *ponum.* The origin of the word *apple* in English is related to old Germanic names for the fruit.

The names of many fruits and vegetables in several languages, including English, reflect the importance of apples, too. In French one name for a tomato is *pomme d'amour,* or love apple. Pineapples and the pomegranates have *apple* and *pomme* in their names. The potato is an "earth apple" in French, Dutch, and German. In Greek myth, sailors sought a golden apple—probably a name for citrons, members of the citrus family.

Apple Roots

The modern-day apple is very different from the tiny, perhaps even poisonous, first apple. This ancient plant developed into the wild crab apple tree, which produced small, tart fruits that people probably didn't eat because of their unpleasant flavor. Although no one knows when, the tasty modern-day apple probably came from mountain slopes in Kazakhstan, which in modern times are thick with flourishing apple trees. Some experts believe that the apple developed south of the Caucasus Mountains in Georgia, Armenia, or Turkey. Central Asian traders could have brought the fruit to Europe. Or the apple might have originated in the Baltics—modern-day Latvia, Lithuania, and Estonia (some geographers include Finland and Poland).

Family Matters

To keep things straight, scientists classify and name living things according to shared features within each of seven major categories. The categories are kingdom, division or phylum, class, order, family, genus, and species. Species share the most features in common, while members of a kingdom or division share far fewer traits. This system of scientific classification and naming is called taxonomy. Scientists refer to plants and animals by a two-part Latin or Greek term made up of the genus and the species name. The genus name comes first, followed by the species name. When talking about a genus, such as apples, that has more than one common species, we'll use only the genus name in the chapter heading. In the discussions about specific fruits, we'll use the two-part species name.

Apple fragments carbon-dated to 6500 B.C. have been found in Turkey. Dried apples have been discovered at Swiss lake dwellings dating back to 6000 B.C. Apples were probably one of the first fruits to be preserved by drying, but some experts think that the apples could have dried naturally. Are the scraps from wild or cultivated fruit trees? No one knows. Although scientists believe that the apple was one of the first cultivated trees, they don't know when the process began.

By 2000 B.C., farmers tended orchards in the fertile Indus River Valley, in what would become India. Egyptians used apples in rituals in 1200 B.C., although no one knows what their version of the apple tasted like. Greek farmers had small orchards by 600 B.C.,

The Legendary Apple

Apples and apple trees pop up in many stories and legends. Merlin the Magician of King Arthur's day sat under an apple tree to help his pupils practice their spells. Snow White's evil stepmother tries to poison her with an apple. Adam and Eve encountered all manner of trouble after eating an apple—the enticing fruit was said to have stuck in Adam's throat. In modern times we refer to the rounded cartilage of the larynx—clearly visible in most men's necks—as the "Adam's apple."

Pliny the Elder

when a people known as the Etruscans began to cultivate apples in what would become Italy. Romans, who ruled the region 500 years later, grew many varieties of apple. At least some of these Roman apples were sweet to the taste. Roman naturalist Pliny the Elder (A.D. 23–79) described 36 varieties. The Api, the apple variety with the longest known history, was first noted at this time. Originally bred by an Etruscan farmer named Appius (whose name has no relation to the word *apple*), this variety of apple was favored by the Romans. In modern times, this same apple variety is enjoyed as *pomme*

Early Storage

Cool, marble-walled rooms in fancy Roman villas were set aside for the storage of apples and other fresh fruit. Another way to keep apples fresh was to place them in wooden boxes, which were then buried in sand. Some people dipped apples in wax or clay, then hung them up in an open courtyard to keep them fresh!

d'Api in France and as the Lady Apple in the United States.

Romans founded an empire—which included much of the Middle East, Europe, and North Africa from 27 B.C. to A.D. 476— and planted orchards across their territory. The Romans brought their apple varieties to Gaul (modern-day France) around 50 B.C. The Gauls interbred the sweet Roman apple varieties with the region's sour native apples. Northern France, known as Normandy, has been big apple-growing country ever since. Hard cider (an alcoholic drink made of fer-

mented apples) became a favorite beverage. And apples grew in northeastern Spain's Basque region. Basque sailors may have learned how to make hard cider from the Gauls in the A.D. 500s. Other experts believe that the Basques introduced hard cider to France long before the Romans arrived in the area.

Apples played a ritual role in Gaul and across the English Channel on the island of Britain. A holiday known as Samhain was a time for picking apples and mistletoe, a flowering, parasitic evergreen plant that grew on apple trees. Samhain also marked the moment for brewing new cider and for drinking down the last of the prior year's batch.

According to legend, the Austrian ruler Gessler ordered William Tell, a Swiss patriot of the fourteenth century, to shoot an arrow through an apple set upon his young son's head. Fortunately Tell succeeded, and after the incident he helped Switzerland gain its independence from Austria.

It's a Fact!

The word for apple is similar in many European languages. All begin with the letter A. The Irish and the Welsh have *abhal* and *afal* from the Celtic *aballo*. The Old English word was *aeppel*. Modern-day Germans say *Apfel*, the word that their ancestors used. Linguists believe that these languages developed from an ancient tongue that had a word like *apple*.

In northern Europe during the Middle Ages (roughly between A.D. 500 and 1500), apples were abundant and cheap. They were tossed into meat stews, used as stuffing for meats, served up as spicy sauces, and, of course, eaten fresh as a snack. A bite of a crisp apple did the work of a toothbrush and toothpaste in those days.

Apples in America

Crab apple trees have grown in North America for untold years. Small and bitter, crab apples weren't good for eating. Native Americans probably did not make much use of them. Cultivated apples came to the Americas with early European settlers. In 1607 the English brought apple seeds to their settlement of Jamestown, Virginia. So did Puritan settlers who, in 1621, arrived at the coast of what would become Massachusetts. John Endecott, the governor of the Puritans' Plymouth Colony, is credited with bringing the first live apple tree to North America. In 1649 Endecott planted 500 apple seedlings, creating what may have been North America's first orchard.

At about the same time, in the Dutch colony of New Amsterdam (which would later become New York City), the governor, Peter Stuyvesant, established a large apple orchard on Manhattan Island's southeast side. By the 1730s, apples from the colonies were exported to British outposts in the West Indies, islands in the Caribbean Sea.

By the mid- to late 1800s, settlers from New England and the Midwest had carried apple trees westward to California and to the southwestern states. German immigrants to South America brought apple trees to Argentina and Chile at about the same time.

Johnny Appleseed

Apple trees have spread across the United States and Canada because of the work of independent nurseries, businesses that specialize in raising and selling the trees.

Born in Leominster, Massachusetts, in 1774, John Chapman spent his life growing apple trees. He founded nurseries across the northeastern and midwestern United States. He bought or rented land for orchards. He planted apple seeds that he had collected from cider mills in the eastern United States. He then sold the seedlings or gave them away.

Chapman lived a simple life. He dressed in worn clothes and often traveled on foot. His energies focused on dispensing young apple trees and helping people in need. His hard work earned Chapman the nickname Johnny Appleseed.

Apples All Over

More than half of the apples that people in the United States eat come from Washington State. Washington's top three international customers are Mexico, Taiwan, and Indonesia. As many as 40,000 workers pick about 12 billion Washington apples every autumn. New York produces 8 percent of the U.S. fresh crop, putting the state a distant second. Michigan supplies 6 percent. California, Pennsylvania, Oregon, and Virginia are also key commercial growers of apples. The island nation of Taiwan usually buys more than 4 million boxes of Washington State Fujis each year. In the 1990s, growers in China planted 4 million acres of apples.

Grafting and Growing

It had been said that apples grow on all but one continent—Antarctica. But apples grow best in temperate regions—areas with warm to hot summers, cool springs and falls, and a chilly winter. Apple trees also grow in tropical areas at high altitudes, where weather is cool.

Apple trees grow easily from seeds. If you drop a seed in good soil, the seed may sprout, grow into a tree, and produce apples. The apples from a seed-grown tree may taste like those from the parent tree. But there is always a chance that the seed might produce a tree with different, unwanted characteristics. In a commercial orchard, growers don't want to risk wasting their energy taking care of a tree that might produce tiny, fragile, or bad-tasting apples. So growers create their apple trees by **grafting**. A graft occurs

Bins of harvested Golden Delicious apples await shipment from orchards in Washington's Yakima Valley.

Growers insert scions (year-old shoots) under the bark of the rootstock *(below),* then fasten them to the rootstock with tape *(right).* Grafting wax covers the top of the rootstock to keep out moisture and disease.

when the living tissues of two trees are bound together, causing them to heal into one tree.

Growers can graft in a number of ways. A common method is to pick one or two shoots of the apple-tree variety that the farmer wants. The grower inserts the shoots into the rootstock—the sawed-off, split base of a strong, healthy seedling. The rootstock is usually chosen for its ability to tolerate bad weather and to resist diseases. Some rootstocks determine the size of the tree. Most rootstock trees are grown from seed—it doesn't matter how their fruit tastes.

A second type of graft is a bud graft. A small section of apple-tree bark containing a bud (a place from which a new shoot will grow) is inserted under the bark of an existing tree. Next the graft is wrapped with tape or rubber bands to hold it together. To protect the operation from rain and insects, the graft is sealed with tape, rubber bands, or grafting wax, which is made from beeswax.

Over the next several weeks, the bud or shoots and the rootstock grow together to make one young tree. Both kinds of grafting are a success if, after two weeks, the buds or shoots show signs of life—they may get plumper or turn green. That's when the wax or tape can be removed.

Planting Apple Trees

Apple growers buy the young grafted trees from nurseries. The growers plant one-year-old trees 20 feet apart in outdoor orchards. For several years, workers must irrigate, fertilize, and prune (trim) young trees as they grow. When the tree is between seven and ten years old, it should begin to produce fruit. Many apple growers decide to plant new orchards with dwarf trees. These bear fruit earlier than do traditional apple trees—usually only three or four years after the seedlings are planted. Also, dwarf trees can be planted as little as four feet apart. This means more apples can be produced per field than in a field of standard trees. Whatever the size, trees and developing apples are regularly sprayed with a series of chemicals to ward off insect attacks and disease.

At this Fuji apple orchard in Washington, young apple trees grow on wire and wood frameworks that provide support for young plants.

Apple blossoms rarely self-pollinate. In fact, most apple trees need to be cross-pollinated with another tree to produce tasty fruit. Just before the apple trees blossom in early spring, workers bring beehives into the orchards. The flowers bloom in clusters and bear pollen (which contains male sperm cells) and nectar. The bees fly to the blossoms to gather the nectar, but at the same time they dust themselves with pollen. When they fly to another tree, they carry the pollen, thereby fertilizing the blossom—which will allow seeds to develop. A fruit will follow. Growers have tried hand pollination and spraying pollen from the air, but bees still do the job best.

Like apple blossoms, apples grow in clusters of four or five. The apple tree can't supply enough nutrients for every apple to continue developing. The tiny, green apples that don't get enough nourishment drop off the branch, usually in June. Farmers call this the June drop. In early summer, workers carefully thin the apples even more, ensuring that the best apples have enough room and nutrients to ripen on the branch.

Some farmers have tried chemical thinning. But the chemicals have side effects, such as killing beneficial insects.

Apple-Pickin' Time

The trees are thick with ripe, delicious fruit by the end of summer. Field workers climb tall ladders to hand-pick the crop. They expertly twist apples off the branch and place the fruit in a shoulder bag. Some workers perch in cherry pickers, which are small cranes that raise the worker to the level of the fruit. Because different

A cluster of apple blossoms in full bloom

Many apple growers use jet-fan sprayers to apply pesticides to their apple trees. This grower wears a gas mask to protect himself from the chemicals.

apple varieties ripen at different times, the harvest can last into October and November.

Workers sort the sacks of picked apples to remove diseased or damaged fruit. Next the fruit is washed and carefully placed in bins, ready for controlled atmosphere storage (CAS). Like all fruits and vegetables, apples take in oxygen and emit carbon dioxide even after the fruit is picked. Because this respiration causes ripening, storage experts limit the oxygen available to the fruit in CAS. Computers monitor air, temperature, and humidity. Apples in CAS can taste fresh even after a year of storage! These apples will be shipped to stores in North America between January and September—the months when apples are not in season. Cold storage can also slow the rate of decay for apples and for other kinds of fruit.

The Wormless Apple

Apples are notoriously wormy—but the fruit that shoppers find at the grocery store is free of apple worms (actually codling moth caterpillars). Female codling moths lay their eggs in apples. The eggs hatch into apple worms. Keeping the apples worm-free has been one reason that apples have been overprotected with **pesticides.** Since 1995 Washington State apple growers have been trying a "pheromone confusion program" to control the codling moth. Male moths find females by their pheromones, natural scents that attract the opposite sex. Scientists reproduced the pheromones in chemical labs. Some growers tie pheromone-filled packets to tree trunks. The male moths hang around the packets instead of mating with the females. This arrangement keeps the apples egg-free.

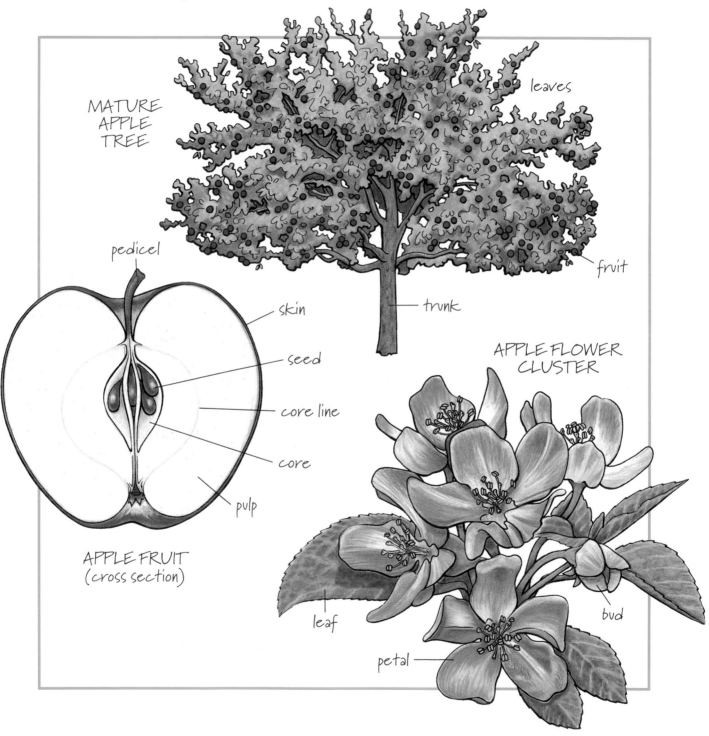

MATURE
APPLE
TREE

leaves

fruit

trunk

pedicel

skin

seed

core line

core

pulp

APPLE FRUIT
(cross section)

APPLE FLOWER
CLUSTER

leaf

petal

bud

To Spray or Not to Spray?

It's a dangerous world for the apple tree—codling moths aren't the only insect that can harm the fruit or tree. More than 500 insects and about 150 diseases assault the apple. Stink bugs and mites are among the bugs. The tree may suffer scab, mildew, and viruses. For years growers have fought back with pesticides, which are chemicals that combat insects, and with herbicides, chemicals aimed at weeds.

Many farmers believe that their high yields and high-quality fruit require the use of chemicals. But some worry about unknown, long-term effects of new chemical products. These materials can affect the soil, bacteria, earthworms, and every other substance in the ground around a treated tree. Chemical residue can eventually enter underground deposits of water, which can lead to polluted drinking water. Chemicals can also run off fields into streams and rivers, which can damage **ecosystems.**

Some apple farmers choose alternatives to large amounts of chemicals. They might use organic farming practices, which reduce or eliminate the use of pesticides and of herbicides. Scientists work to breed varieties of apple trees that they hope will resist insects, diseases, and cold weather. Integrated Pest Management (IPM) is another new approach. IPM can mean using harmless bugs to fight insects that harm trees.

Name Your Poison

From the 1890s to the 1940s, arsenic (a poison deadly to humans) was a favorite pesticide to spray on apple trees. In 1945 dichloro-diphenyl-trichloroethane (DDT) became the preferred pesticide of apple growers. DDT has been blamed for the huge rise in a range of cancers among Americans. DDT has also been linked to birth defects, infertility, and other maladies. DDT was banned in the 1960s. Alar, a chemical that helped apples stay on the tree until ripe, was the subject of concern in 1989. A study indicated that Alar caused cancerous tumors in mice. When traces of Alar turned up in apple juice, public outrage caused the manufacturer to remove the product from the market. Subsequent investigations into Alar have had mixed results. Some findings show the chemical to be harmless, but others support its removal.

Varieties and Names

Always shiny and usually round, apples come in red, green, and yellow. Some combine the colors with stripes.

The apple's firm flesh ranges in color from white to cream to yellow, and its seeds lie together in a core. The taste of the fruit can be tart or sweet.

A hurricane that devastated Virginia in 1969 prompted the discovery of a tasty new apple variety, the Ginger Gold. After the storm passed, apple growers Clyde and Ginger Harvey found a tiny, new apple tree in their orchard. It was unlike the other trees that grew there. By the 1980s, nursery workers who had nurtured the tree realized that it produced a new, spicy apple. The new apple variety was promptly named after Ginger Harvey and for the golden color of the fruit.

Plant breeders regularly cross one apple with another to see if their offspring makes an unusual new fruit. Testing such crosses takes years but may give the world a tasty new variety of apple. The Empire was created by breeding a Macintosh, a relatively tart apple, with Red Delicious, an extremely sweet one.

Japanese breeders have produced the Fuji apple, named for their country's distinctive volcanic mountain. To make the Fuji, breeders used Red Delicious and an heirloom apple called the Ralls Janet. The Fuji has broken records for its longevity at room temperature. Another Japanese apple is the Mutsu, a green apple the British renamed Crispin. The Granny Smith is a well-known, bright green apple that came from New South Wales in southern Australia. It bears the name of a woman named Mrs. Smith, who first grew it in 1868. These days Chile and Australia grow lots of Granny Smiths.

Apples of different shapes, sizes, and colors can be grown in the same orchard.

To Your Health!

"An apple a day keeps the doctor away" is an old saying that really has merit! High in fiber, apples help intestinal function. The fruit is also low in fat and is a source of potassium. That helps the body use fluids. Apples also contain pectin, a fiber that helps to maintain even blood sugar levels. Pectin may help lower blood cholesterol levels. Apple crunching may also clean your teeth, keeping cavities at bay.

Most apple cider is perfectly safe to drink. But in 1996, a batch of U.S. cider that contained *Escherichia coli* (E. coli) bacteria killed one person and made dozens ill. The apple press that made the cider had been placed close to fecal matter (which carries the dangerous bacteria). Many cider mills have installed pasteurization equipment to prevent contamination. Pasteurization kills off virtually all bacteria, but it can also destroy the tangy taste that makes cider different from mere apple juice.

Not all apple varieties become world famous—each apple area has its particular local favorites that munchers enjoy each season. French people love the Calville. The British prefer Cox's Orange Pippin, Italians choose the Abondanza, and Belgians often choose the Boskoop.

Saucy!

Whether in someone's kitchen or in a giant processing plant, the basic idea behind making applesauce is much the same. Chopped apples are boiled until the fruit is soft—that's how it is done.

A large apple-processing company usually makes sauce in the fall, when apples are harvested. The apples arrive packed in large, wooden crates, which are emptied into tanks where the fruit is washed. A water canal carries the clean apples to the area set aside for peeling. Along the way, workers cull (pull from the canal) unsuitable apples. A device peels and cores the fruit. Inspectors make sure that the apples are cleaned of chemicals and are ready to be cooked before the fruit is

E. coli bacteria live in everyone's intestine, but when ingested can lead to infections.

tossed into an airtight steam cooker. Machines press cooked apples through a screen to remove any seeds and stems that were not cored out. At this point, sweeteners or spices might be added to make flavored applesauces. Chopped, cooked apples are stirred into the creamy blend to make chunky style.

The hot applesauce is ladled into jars or into individual plastic cups, where it is then sealed and cooled. After cooling, the containers are labeled, packed into cartons, and shipped to stores and warehouses.

Juicing the Apple

People have been drinking juiced apples for thousands of years. Unfiltered, tangy apple juice, called cider, was drunk fresh or allowed to ferment slightly into hard cider. In winter hard cider can be set outdoors until it's partially frozen. People pick out the ice, and the remaining liquid is a fiery drink called applejack. If hard cider is left at room temperature a little longer, the alcohol turns into sour vinegar. Decades ago small farms had cider presses. Communities had large cider mills.

Cider mills or presses differ, but juice is always the result. In some places, mill workers wash apples twice before putting them through a hammer mill, a crushing device that turns apples into a pulpy mass. Then the pulp is placed in a series of trays. Usually a wooden or stone plate presses the pulp flat,

In earlier days, people made apple juice using a hand-operated cider press that crushed apples into a pulp and then squeezed the juice into a bucket. To operate the press, a person turned the crank.

thereby releasing the apples' juice. Cider makers operate the press with a lever or by turning a handle.

Apples with Everything

People eat apples baked, stewed, grated, and dried. North Americans eat apple muffins and apple pie, baked apples with cream, apples stewed with raisins, apple dumplings, applesauce, apple cake, apple fritters, apple pancakes, and apple butter.

In Denmark cooks stuff pork loins with chopped apples and prunes. Some fill the Christmas goose with the same mix. Shredded apples in a bowl of fresh whipped cream make a light, rich salad. Muffins are made with pastry dough, chopped apples, a dollop of apricot preserves, and slivered almonds. In Sweden diners eat Canadian bacon, sautéed onions, and apples for Sunday breakfast. Baked apples with sour cherries are a German favorite for dessert, as is apple pudding. Turks customarily eat raw apples after fish dishes. Israelis favor tart applesauce made from green apples.

Dig In!

MULLED APPLE CIDER
(7 CUPS)

1 teaspoon whole allspice
2 quarts apple cider or apple juice
2 cinnamon sticks
⅔ cups firmly packed brown sugar
14 whole cloves
Ground nutmeg to taste

Place the allspice, cinnamon sticks, and cloves in a small cheesecloth bag and tie it firmly. Pour the cider and the sugar into a large saucepan. Add the spice bag. Simmer for 15 minutes over low heat (longer if a spicier flavor is desired). Remove the spice bag. Serve the hot, mulled cider in mugs. Sprinkle the nutmeg on top!

Peaches

[Prunus persica]

The peach tree grows wild in China, where it has been cultivated since 400 B.C. and possibly earlier. The peach was considered to be so lovely and close to perfection that it was a symbol of immortality. According to Chinese legend, a person who ate peaches would avoid death and aging. But few peach trees live more than 20 years—a short life span for a tree—so the symbolism is puzzling. In modern-day China, the gift of a porcelain or fresh peach indicates affection.

Persian traders from what would become Iran were probably the first to bring the peach and other exotic goods from China to the Middle East, but historians are unable to date the event. History also is hazy as to when the Greeks and Romans encountered the fruit in Persia. They thought that was where it had originated, so the Romans called the fruit the *malus persicum,* or Persian apple.

Peaches hang from the branch of a peach tree at a Washington State orchard.

Today I ate a white peach from the Farmer's Market. I was at a serious gathering, and nevertheless, the juice spilled over my chin and onto my yellow shirt.

—Mary Helen Snyder

This Roman fresco, or wall painting, of a half-eaten peach dates to the Roman Empire.

By about 50 B.C., Romans cultivated peaches in Gaul on a small scale. Although they raised some peaches, by the first century A.D., Romans imported most of their peaches from Persia. A fresco from this period in Herculaneum, a Roman town in southern Italy, shows a half-eaten peach.

The peach struggled in the fields until the Middle Ages. The cool summers and too-cold winters were not friendly to peach trees, which are sensitive to chilly weather. In about A.D. 800, Moors (from North Africa) conquered the Iberian Peninsula (modern-day Spain and Portugal), bringing peaches with them. But European peach trees didn't produce their best fruit until grown in special greenhouses and walled gardens.

Peaches in America

Many years later, Spaniards arriving in Mexico in the 1520s and in Florida in the 1560s brought peach trees to the Americas. The trees flourished, and the fruit was popular with Native Americans. The Natchez people of Florida named one of the months in their calendar after the peach. The local Creeks and the Seminoles were also peach fans. In 1663 William Penn, the founder of Pennsylvania, wrote an enthusiastic letter about the peach trees cultivated by Native Americans. By the early 1700s, unknown travelers had brought the peach to Georgia, where it became a staple crop. Regional growers developed new peach varieties that made the state a peach power after the 1860s.

Peach Ball

During World War II, men's professional baseball came to a halt as ballplayers joined the army. A league of women players, called the All American Girls Professional Baseball League, filled the gap. In 1943 a team called the Rockford Peaches was founded. Based in Rockford, Illinois, the team played until the league was dissolved in 1954.

By the late 1800s, Georgians made the Elberta peach the most famous variety in the country. These days Georgians grow more than 40 varieties of peaches. The state's orchards boast about 2.5 million peach trees. Fresh, delicious Georgia peaches, anticipated by true fans nationwide, are available for only 12 weeks every spring. And the peach is a source of local pride. Georgia's slogan is The Peach State. It claims college football's Peach Bowl in Atlanta, where more than 40 streets are named Peachtree.

But believe it or not, Georgia isn't the leader in U.S. peach production. Bringing in about 700 million pounds of peaches a year, California far surpasses both Georgia and its nearby rival, South Carolina. In both South Carolina and Georgia, peach production was devastated by a freeze in 1996, so their combined peach poundage came to only 13 million that year. They bounced back in 1997 with about 160 million pounds each.

The Georgia peach industry thrived during the late 1800s. In this picture, orchard workers proudly display the fruits of their labor.

Elberta, You're a Peach . . . .

In the 1870s and for many years after, the Elberta peach was the U.S. favorite. The full-flavored, attractive, and sturdy Elberta was developed by Samuel H. Rumph, a Georgia native. Rumph created the new peach by experimenting with a Chinese Cling peach tree. He promptly named the tasty fruit after his wife, Elberta. The first variety of peach to be shipped to New York City, the Elberta was a success. In fact it sparked the Georgia peach industry.

The seed inside a tough peach pit looks like an almond. Unlike almonds, peach seeds contain naturally occurring chemicals called cyanogenic glycocides. In the intestines, these substances produce cyanide, a dangerous poison.

Cling or Free, What'll It Be?

Peaches come in hundreds of varieties. Their fuzzy skins range in color from yellow to red, with either yellow or white flesh. Inside the tough peach pit (also called a stone) is a slender seed that resembles an almond. This is no surprise, for the peach and the almond are close cousins. Like the apple, both are members of Rosaceae, the huge rose family. Peaches grow on short trees—about 20 to 25 feet tall—that resemble fragile willows. The leaves are slender and tooth-edged. In addition to their delicious fruit, peach trees are cherished for the extraordinary beauty of their sweetly scented blossoms.

Peaches come in many varieties but in two major types—freestone and cling. The freestone peaches have flesh that easily separates from the inner seed. Clingstone peach flesh, contrastingly, clings to the stone. Freestones generally are for fresh market sale. Chile provides 99 percent of all the fresh, freestone peaches imported to the United States. Most clingstone peaches are canned. Greece, a major provider of canned clingstone peaches to the United States, sup-

Set between rows of blooming peach trees are heaters called smudge pots, which help prevent frost. Cold can prevent a peach bud *(inset)* from opening and can even kill a peach tree.

plied 41 percent of the U.S. import total in 1997. Spain was close behind with 39 percent, and South Africa took third place.

Planting, Picking, and Packing Peaches

Most peach trees are the product of grafts. Commercial growers buy grafted trees from nurseries and then plant the trees in furrows made by a tractor. In times past, peach trees were planted 20 feet apart to give them room to reach their full height. These days growers try to pack more trees onto the same parcel of land to increase fruit production. Shorter, radically pruned trees make this possible. Where once 108 trees per acre were planted, today that figure could reach 1,000.

Three or four years after planting, peach trees put out fruit. The trees are well weeded, pruned, and watered along the way. Not all young peach trees are just planted and left to grow. Some commercial peach orchards prefer to train fruit trees to grow against a wall or a **trellis.** The trees are espaliered—spread against trellises with their branches tied horizontally from their trunks. That may not look comfortable for the tree, but the results are impressive. The peaches receive more light and grow plumper than average fruit. Espaliered trees can be planted closer together and the fruit is easy to pick.

When the peaches are ripe but still hard to the touch, workers climb short ladders to pick the easily bruised fruit. They place it in

Unlike peaches destined for canning, peaches to be sold fresh must be handled carefully so they don't bruise. Tree-ripened peaches are harvested when ripe but still firm.

canvas bags worn on the chest or in buckets that they carry with them. They transfer the fresh crop into boxes. Others load the boxes into trucks and drive them to cold storage, where workers sort and grade the peaches. In storage the fruit is cooled to ensure that it will reach the marketplace before the ripening finishes.

Canning peaches get rougher treatment. The ripe fruit is occasionally harvested with a tree shaker. As the shaker does its work, a canvas contraption surrounding the tree catches the falling fruit, which then goes into a truck. The fruit is graded and taken to a processing plant, where the peaches are washed and their skins dissolved with chemicals. Machines pit the fruit, slice it, and either freeze it or put it in cans with sugary syrup or water. The cans are steamed in vats of boiling water, then sealed and packed into boxes ready for shipment to stores and warehouses.

It's a Fact!

Dust can bring pesky insects to peach orchards. So peach pits often end up back in the orchards, where workers spread them over roads and paths to keep down the dust. After processing, a small amount of flesh remains on the pit. That allows the pits to adhere to one another on the roadbed. The resulting pavement is surprisingly durable. Growers usually add a new layer of pits to the roads each year.

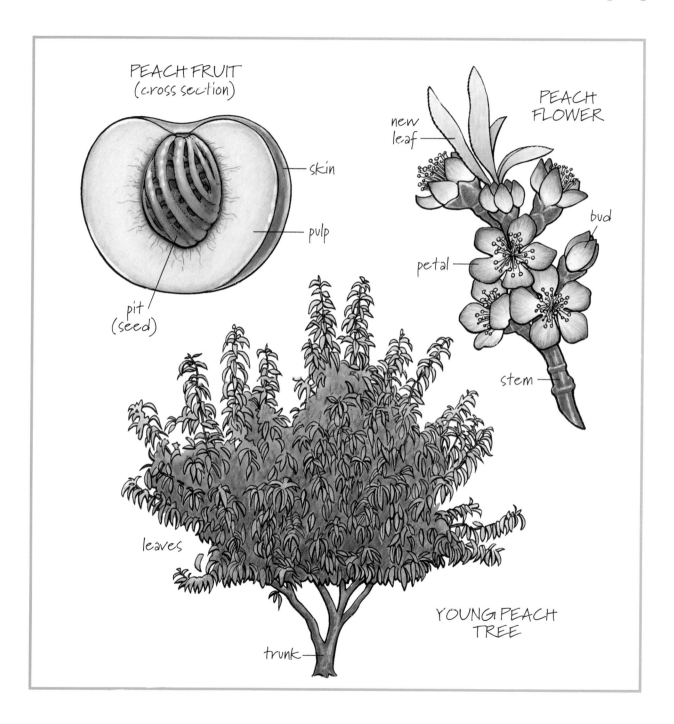

PEACH FRUIT
(cross section)

skin

pulp

pit
(seed)

PEACH
FLOWER

new
leaf

bud

petal

stem

leaves

YOUNG PEACH
TREE

trunk

Dig In!

PEACH COBBLER
(8 SERVINGS)

6 peaches
⅓ cup sugar
⅔ cup flour
1½ teaspoons baking powder
⅔ cup skim milk
2 tablespoons melted butter
Cinnamon and sugar to taste

Mix the dry ingredients together. Add the milk and stir the blend with a whisk until smooth. Wash, peel, pit, and slice the peaches. Put the melted butter into a large casserole or baking dish. Pour in the batter and place the sliced peaches on top.

Sprinkle the cinnamon and a bit of sugar on top. Bake at 350° until the dish just begins to brown. Serve warm. Try it with a scoop of vanilla ice cream on top!

To easily peel off the peach's fuzzy skin, dip the peach into boiling water for about 30 seconds. Then dip into cold water. The skin should slide right off. Slice and eat.

Peckish for Peaches

As with most fruits, peaches are often eaten fresh. But that's only one of many choices. You can slice peaches and then sprinkle sugar on top. Or top a biscuit with a slice of the fruit and add a dollop of fresh whipped cream to make peach shortcake. Or bake peaches into pies and make peach cobblers. Peaches flavor delicious ice cream and aromatic vinegar, too.

In the 1800s, a famous French chef created a dessert called *pêche Melba*, named for Nellie Melba, a popular Australian opera singer. Known in English as peach Melba, the dish features (poached) peaches on vanilla ice cream, topped with raspberry sauce. Around the world, peaches are chopped into fruity salsas, sliced into fruit salads, and mixed with vegetables in curries. Mexicans use the fruit to make rich confections, such as candied peaches. Also in Mexico, peaches add flavor to stews and to other main dishes.

Poaching is a method of cooking foods slowly in a liquid that is hot but not boiling.

Workers at a processing plant inspect peaches as they come tumbling down a conveyor belt. All peaches must be inspected before the canning process begins. The clingstone variety of peach is most often used for canning.

To Your Health!

Peaches pack more than pits—they are full of vitamin A, which aids healthy eyesight and helps the body to resist certain cancers. Peaches also have moderate amounts of fiber.

Mangoes
[Mangifera indica]

Eating a fresh, juicy mango is an exquisite experience in stickiness. The flesh clings to a huge, flat seed, and it can be difficult to remove. And some mangoes are threaded with fibers. But the mango's delicious flavor is well worth the effort. This fruit is sweet, brightly colored, and refreshing.

In India the mango is a symbol of love and a granter of wishes. Mango leaves are featured at weddings. Legend has it that the leaves will ensure that newly married couples are able to bear children. When a baby is born, villagers celebrate by decorating doorways with mango leaves.

People sometimes refer to the mango as the king of tropical fruits.

The mangoes are glad to be stuck in the teeth.

—Richard Tipping

A fruit vendor in India, which produces more mangoes than any other country in the world, displays a cartload of mangoes for customers.

Mango Beginnings

Thousands of years ago, the mango originated in an area overlapping what would become India and Myanmar—Asian countries that border the Indian Ocean. The mango tree was probably flourishing in the fertile Indus River Valley by 4000 B.C. But for a long time, the mango didn't venture far from its place of origin. The fruit is highly perishable, and its seed decays quickly. Because of this, people didn't carry mangoes with them on long-distance trading missions.

Only gradually did the mango tree spread across the tropics. A Chinese scribe named Hwen T'sang mentioned mangoes in the A.D. 600s. By 1000 Persian traders had introduced the tree to Africa, and three centuries later Europeans wrote of the fruit. Portuguese growers raised mango trees in Brazil in the eighteenth century. By the 1740s, mangoes grew on Caribbean islands, in Australia, in New Zealand, and across southern Africa.

Mangoes in Modern Times

Mangoes arrived in Florida in the 1820s, and planters were raising them in the Miami area by the 1850s. A Florida-bred mango called Haden was the local favorite because of its lack of fibers. Florida's mango production increased steadily until 1992, when Hurricane Andrew blew down hundreds of mango trees. But growers were undaunted. In 1998 Florida mango production was 5.5 million. It increases each year. These days, growers favor mangoes of the Tommy Atkins and Keitt varieties.

In the 1990s, Hawaiian growers planted about 7,400 mango trees on what had once been sugarcane acreage on Oahu's north shore. The harvest serves the local Hawaiian market and sells for less than imported mangoes.

The young mango tree sometimes grows in huge spurts of one foot at a time.

A young boy in the Central African Republic reaches for a fresh, green mango.

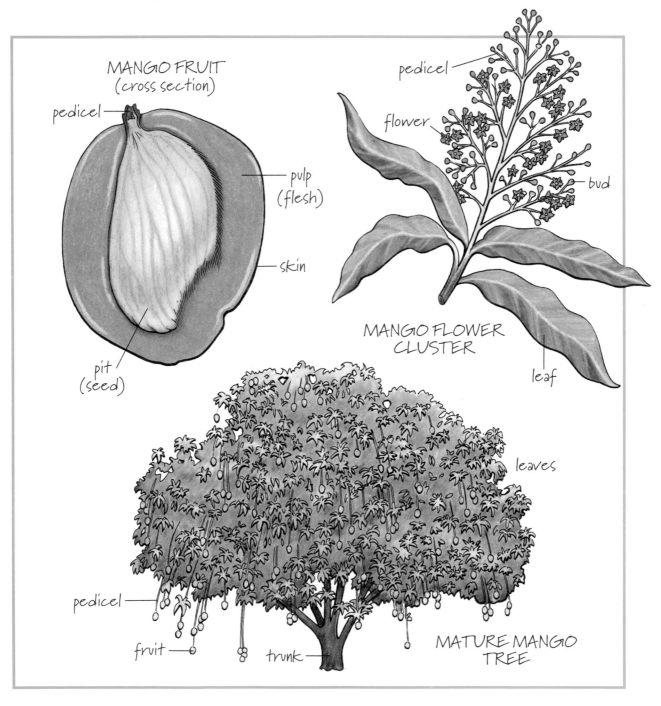

MANGO FRUIT
(cross section)

pedicel

pulp
(flesh)

skin

pit
(seed)

MANGO FLOWER
CLUSTER

pedicel

flower

bud

leaf

leaves

pedicel

fruit

trunk

MATURE MANGO
TREE

Growing

Mangoes come in many shapes, colors, and sizes. Kidney-shaped, oval, or round, mangoes can be two inches around and weigh about two ounces. Or they might grow as large as ten inches and weigh a hefty five pounds. The tough, leathery skin of most mangoes is green with rosy highlights, but mangoes might have a yellow, red, or purple peel. The flesh is always an exuberant orange, and it ranges in texture from stringy to tender and juicy.

Although mangoes are traditionally grown from seed, many commercial growers around the world have turned to grafting. As with all fruit-tree grafts, this ensures that the fruit will taste the way that the grower expects. About four years after being grafted, a mango tree can begin to bear fruit. Mangoes in nature only fruit every other year, but with careful pruning, growers can usually have an annual harvest.

Mango trees are tropical evergreens (they don't lose their leaves) that can grow to be 60 feet tall. Planters usually set mango trees about 45 feet apart. Florida's mango groves are filled with smaller trees—between 20 and 25 feet tall—placed about 30 feet apart.

The tree requires consistent irrigation before it puts out its pink, star-shaped blossoms. So in Florida, underground pipes steadily release drips of water. But when the fruit begins to form, the tree requires little water, so it can flourish even in summertime droughts. Between 15 and 20 weeks after flowering, the mangoes are ready to pick. Mango harvesting can last from May until August, as not all of the fruit ripens at the same time.

The fruit of the mango tree develops from the ovaries of its blossoms.

It's a Fact!

Turpentine is a substance derived from pine trees and often used as paint thinner. Certain varieties of mangoes have an intense turpentine odor on the skin and in the sap that can gather around the stem. The variety named Turpentine certainly does. But its interior fruit remains sweet and spicy.

A mango pit is wide and flat, and removing the flesh from the seed can be tricky.

Picking Mangoes

When mangoes are full size and of the proper color but still firm to the touch, the harvest begins. Pickers pluck mangoes daily when the fruit is in season, which varies from region to region. In South Africa, workers use long poles topped with shears to clip off the fruit. A bag attached to the pole catches the fruit. In Florida workers perch in cherry pickers to pick the fruit.

Many growers plan for their mangoes to be eaten fresh. These fruits are washed in water and then in a fungicide, which prevents the fruit from getting moldy. Then the mangoes are packed by size. Some mangoes are destined to become juice. They're sent through a machine that removes the peel and seed. The fruit is squished through a filter. The resulting juice is

Step one

Step two

Step three

How to Slice a Mango

Slicing a mango can be messy without this trick. Find a kitchen knife, a ripe mango, and a cutting board. You may want to ask an adult to help you.

Step one: Cut off the mango's "cheeks." Slice each side about half an inch from an imaginary line down the center of the mango. Make the cut as close to the seed as possible so that you get most of the fruit.

Step two: Using the tip of the knife, carefully score each cheek of the mango. Cut through the flesh to—but not through—the skin. Step three: Pick up each piece and push on the skin as if to turn it inside out. You can pick chunks of mango off the pushed-out skin.

If you like, you can peel the middle of the mango—the part with the seed—and bite off the rest of the fruit.

pasteurized before it is ready for the market. To make canned mangoes, processors peel and slice the fruit. Next processors pop it into cans with a sugar syrup. Other mangoes are sliced, treated with a preservative, and dried. The dried mangoes are usually sealed in airtight packages before being shipped to markets across the world.

A Popular Treat

These days mangoes thrive around the world. India grows millions of tons of the fruit on over two million acres of land. Brazil and Colombia are major exporters of mangoes, particularly to Europe. Mexico and South Africa grow and export mangoes. Malaysia and West African countries with tropical climates are great mango growers, but they export little of the fruit.

All Florida-grown mangoes are eaten in the United States. U.S. mango consumption has jumped by 20 percent each year since 1993. American fruit eaters now regularly choose mangoes over apricots, cherries, and plums. To meet the demand, the United States imported more than 311 million pounds of mangoes from Mexico in 1996. Haiti, Guatemala, and Brazil also export mangoes to North America.

Ten percent of South Africa's production is exported, primarily to the Netherlands. Over half of what South Africa grows is made into *achar,* a sauce of green (unripe) mango, vegetables, and hot spices. Another ten percent of the crop is made into juice.

Chutneys are spicy condiments containing fruit and vinegar.

To Your Health!

Mangoes are rich in beta-carotene, a component of vitamin A that is crucial to healthy eyes and skin. Beta-carotene works to combat cancer. Mangoes also contain minerals, including potassium, zinc, and magnesium.

Munching on Mangoes

The world over, fresh mangoes make delicious snacks—by themselves or sliced into salads. Many are made into refreshing drinks by blending the juicy fruit with coconut milk or with other tropical fruits. In the Caribbean, mangoes turn up in desserts like mousses and pies. Mango chutneys are a delicious treat, too.

Cooks in Malaysia know that green mangoes contain an enzyme that helps to tenderize meat. They marinate the raw meat in mango pulp and juice. Malaysian cooks add green mangoes to vegetable dishes. Coconut-

Dig In!

AAM RAS (MANGO DESSERT)
(4 SERVINGS)

5 cups mango pulp, fresh or canned
1 cup cream or half-and-half
Seeds of 3 green cardamom pods, crushed,
   or 1/4 to 1/2 teaspoon ground cardamom
Sugar to sprinkle on top

If using fresh mangoes, remove the skin and slice into a bowl. Crush the cardamom seeds in a mortar and pestle. If you don't have one, put the seeds on a cutting board. Roll a heavy jar over the seeds, pressing down to crush them. Put the mango pulp, cream, and seeds into a blender. Combine on high for a few seconds. Then pour mixture into a bowl and chill in the refrigerator. Sprinkle with sugar before serving.

flavored sticky rice with mangoes is a classic Thai dish. Indians eat a vegetable curry with mango and banana slices. They also enjoy a curry made with coconut, chilies, and mango. Dried mangoes are a popular flavoring used in Indian cuisine. Latin Americans enjoy mango paste served with mild white cheese.

Figs

[Ficus carica]

The fig is a fruit that people love or hate. To some it tastes too sweet. To others it is the finest of treats, rare because of the difficulty growing it in most climates. Fig trees grow about 30 feet high and feature deep green leaves that resemble human hands. Figs are small and pear-shaped or oval. They come in a rainbow of skin colors, from green to yellow, from pink to purple, and from brown to black.

Fig trees don't produce traditional flowers. Instead the part of the fig that is considered the fruit contains the tree's tiny flowers within it. The flowers become the hard seeds that give a fig its crunch.

Crunchy, sweet figs have an extremely high sugar content.

*Let the world slide,
let the world go;
A fig for care
and a fig for woe!*

—John Heywood

Figs were an important source of food for people in ancient times. The thin-skinned and easily bruised fruit was either eaten fresh from the tree or was dried and stored. The fig probably originated in Asia Minor, in what would become Turkey. The fruit's written history dates back to 3,000 B.C., when it was mentioned in the Sumerian epic of Gilgamesh. Ancient Assyrians of this era, living in what would become Iraq, evidently used fig syrup as a sweetener. Their neighbors living in Babylonia between the Tigris and Euphrates Rivers planted figs in the city's legendary hanging gardens.

Ancient Egyptians were fig growers and placed the fruit in tombs. Experts think that the figs may have been intended as a snack for the afterlife. The Phoenicians were merchants from the Middle East who grew and sold figs. They may have established the fig from North Africa to the Iberian Peninsula by 700 B.C.

The Bible describes Adam and Eve wearing fig leaves. Throughout the Bible, figs are mentioned as an important crop. Early Greek farmers honored Demeter, their goddess of farming, by planting groves of fig trees in her name. Greek athletes included the fruit in their training diets. And Olympic victors received the finest figs along with their laurel leaf crowns. In fact, some experts believe that the crowns were woven of fig leaves. Attica, the area of Greece that included the city-state of Athens, was a fig-exporting power. By the seventh century B.C., locals worried that there would be no figs left for the Athenians to enjoy. Rulers enacted laws restricting the sale of figs abroad.

Even so, by 200 B.C., Greek figs were on their way to India and Rome, where they became important crops. The wealthiest Romans preferred figs imported from the Greek islands and from Syria. As the Roman Empire grew, the soldiers brought figs with them to regions such as Gaul. The Romans believed that Bacchus, their god of wine, had brought them the fig. His followers adorned

Bacchus, the Roman god of wine, as portrayed by the Italian artist Caravaggio

Fig-Fat Geese

The Greeks, the Gauls, and the Romans force-fed figs to geese. Why? They believed that a sweet, rich diet of figs ensured a plump liver, which was required for the delicacy known as pâté de foie gras. *Foie gras* translates from French to mean "fat liver," but English speakers usually refer to the delicacy as pâté.

his statues with fig leaves on special days. But they had down-to-earth reasons for loving the sweet fruit, too. Roman naturalist and writer Pliny the Elder praised the fig as a healthy food—even claiming that elderly fig fans would look less wrinkly. Figs stayed popular in Europe. Citizens of Lutetia (later Paris, France) carefully tended the fig trees that grew in the nearby countryside. In the A.D. 300s, future Roman emperor Julian (ca. 331–363) noted that "they take care to wrap round with straw or some other covering to protect them from bad weather."

In the A.D. 700s, Arabs carried improved varieties of figs from Egypt across North Africa and northward into Spain and Portugal. The Algarve region of Portugal became famous for its figs. For many northern Mediterranean peoples, the fig was a vital part of their diets. Bakers made dried figs into bread. Some people used figs to make a wine.

In the 1300s, Parisian diners enjoyed fig desserts. Puddings in sixteenth-century England were regularly made of dried figs. The treats were immortalized in the Christmas carol "We Wish You a Merry Christmas," in which singers demand "figgy pudding."

Figs across the World

Spaniards carried figs from Seville, Spain, to the Caribbean Islands and South America in the 1520s. Forty years later, Florida and Mexico probably received the fig from Spaniards. In 1575 travelers carried figs from Cuba to the coast of what became South Carolina. The trees arrived in gardens of Jamestown, Virginia, by 1621. French settlers planted figs in Louisiana, which in the 1720s was a French territory

Holy Tree

An East Indian fig, the bo tree, plays a role in Buddhism.

Prince Siddhartha Gautama was a wealthy Indian nobleman who renounced all worldly goods. He passed many hours deep in thought under a huge bo tree. He believed that people could become completely happy and at peace. He also believed in a cycle of death and rebirth. When he had achieved wisdom, he became known as Buddha and his followers as Buddhists. The religion has millions of believers around the world.

In Sri Lanka, the ruins of an ancient city boasts a tree that was planted about 288 B.C. According to legend, the tree grew from a cutting from Buddha's fig tree.

that spread from the Mississippi River to the Rocky Mountains. Beginning in 1759, Spanish priests planted figs from San Diego to Sonoma, California, wherever they founded a mission (a religious settlement where the priests tried to convert Native Americans to Christianity). The dark purple Mission fig stems from that time.

In 1769 the renowned gardener and future U.S. president Thomas Jefferson noted the first fig planting at his home, Monticello. He chose a south-facing spot protected by garden walls. This sheltered growing area created a warm place where the fig trees flourished. Throughout the southern United States, fig trees were planted as sturdy hedges, which in modern days mark the sites where eighteenth-century dwellings stood.

Figs loved the warm dry weather of California's San Joachin Valley. The first commercial orchards were established there in the 1850s. Full commercial fig production was underway by 1900. In modern times, California grows about 20 percent of the world's figs and virtually all figs commercially raised in the United States.

Growing a Fig Tree

Commercial fig trees come from cuttings—small twigs or branches cut from an established tree. Tree nursery workers place the cuttings indoors in water or in moist soil, where the little branches sprout roots to become new trees. When the new trees are one year old, growers plant them in orchards. Most farmers set the saplings about 20 feet apart, 155 trees to an acre. Fig growers regularly prune the tree's branches throughout the tree's life. The young fig tree begins bearing fruit when between 5 and 7 years of age. An average-sized fig tree is 15 to 20 feet tall and can produce between 40 and 50 pounds of figs every year.

Fertilizing a Fig Tree

Most flowering plants produce blooms with both male and female parts. Fig trees have either male or female flowers. Certain varieties of fig trees produce fruit without external pollination. But some varieties need to be pollinated. Farmers may cut branches from a

As the fig develops, it becomes large and fleshy. Fig trees produce two or three crops of fruit each year.

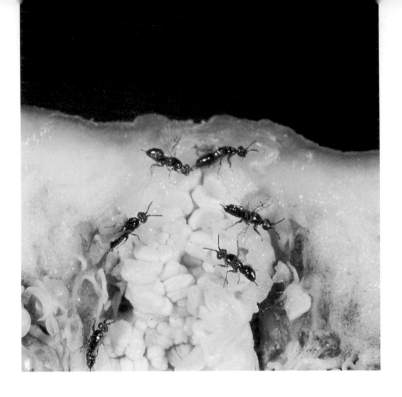

A close-up of fig wasps inside a fig. Fig wasps carry pollen from the flowers of a wild fig to the flowers of the Smyrna fig. The Smyrna fig requires the pollen to bear fruit.

male tree and hang them in an orchard full of female trees so that fertilization can take place.

Other types of fig trees can be pollinated only by a tiny female fig wasp *(Blastophaga psenes)*, which is born, lays eggs, and then dies on the same day. Male and female wasps hatch from eggs deposited inside the inedible figs of a male tree. A male wasp hatched in one of the fig's flowers seeks a female born in another. He gnaws open her flower, fertilizes her, and dies—without ever leaving the male fig. That's when the female wasp exits the fig, her body covered with pollen.

The female wasp flies to another fig. If it is a female fig, the wasp is out of luck—only a male fig is compatible with her egg-laying gear. She may fly to many different fig trees on her search, and each time she leaves behind some pollen from the male fig tree. That pollen fertilizes the female figs, which allows them to ripen into fruit. Finally the wasp dies—whether or not she laid her eggs.

It's a Fact!

American military personnel involved in the 1991 Gulf War carried survival bars made of figs. The recipe had been in development for three years. Figs were chosen to be a key ingredient because of their high calcium and low fat.

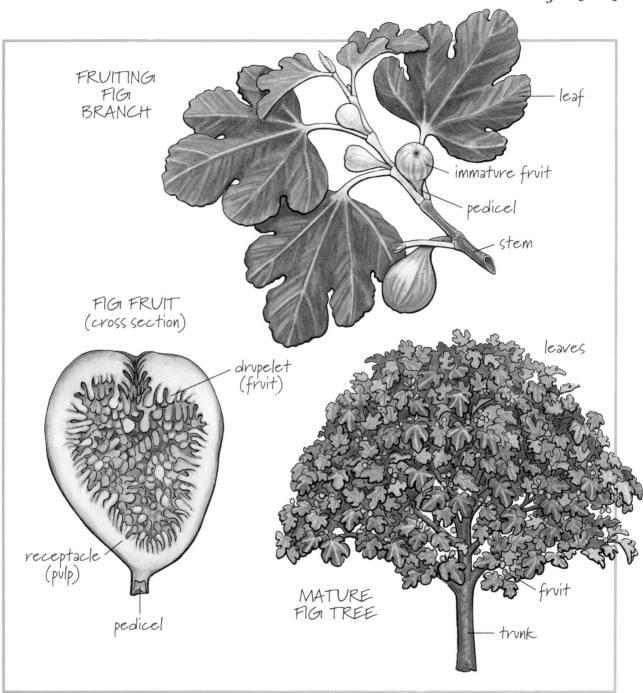

FRUITING
FIG
BRANCH

leaf

immature fruit

pedicel

stem

FIG FRUIT
(cross section)

drupelet
(fruit)

receptacle
(pulp)

pedicel

leaves

MATURE
FIG TREE

fruit

trunk

Fig trees, like this one in the African nation of Tanzania, thrive in hot sun and can live for centuries.

Farmers take advantage of the female wasps' determination. They plant groves of female fig trees (other, smaller groves of male trees are usually nearby to allow the cycle to continue). When it is time for the figs to be pollinated, the farmers pick wasp-filled male figs and place them in bags, which are hung in the groves of female trees.

Fig Harvesting

California's Mission figs produce two crops a year. The first crop, in late June, is used for fresh figs and for fig paste—a product that processors use to make cakes, cookies, and bars. Workers pick them by hand when the fruit's flesh is still firm to the touch. Pickers climb ladders against the trees and wear gloves to protect their hands from the sticky resin released by the fruit's stem as it is twisted off the tree. The fruit is placed in buckets, transferred quickly to cold storage, then shipped to stores or to canneries.

The second crop ripens in late summer and partially dries on the tree. Figs to be sold dry are harvested from the tree and off the ground. Therefore the ground that surrounds the trees must be kept flat, smooth, and weed-free. Sometimes workers use rollers to maintain a surface as smooth as a tennis court. Fully ripe figs fall to the ground, where they dry some more. A worker drives a mechanical harvester that sweeps up figs. It separates out any leaves, sticks, or debris before it pours the figs into large bins in the grower's outdoor dry yard. Here the partially dry figs are laid out in large, flat trays. After a few days in the sunshine, the figs are very dry.

Inspectors evaluate figs from each tray to ensure that they meet growers' standards. Then the figs are set on a conveyor belt, where they are washed, sorted, and graded by size. Unless they are needed for immediate processing, figs are put back in plastic bins, which are moved to cold storage.

Some spend 12 hours bathed with hot circulating air in a dehydrator. After all the drying to which figs are subjected, it may seem odd that they are remoisturized in processing. Moisture content of the dried figs is

Figs boast over 600 varieties around the world.

Trays of figs dry in the sun at a fig orchard in South Africa. Because ripe figs spoil easily, many growers dry their figs before shipping.

To Your Health!

Figs are full of sugar, as you might guess from their sweet taste. But they also carry a powerful punch of calcium, a mineral that helps to maintain strong bones and teeth. In fact, a fig has as much calcium as half a glass of milk. Figs are also high in fiber and carry a significant amount of iron, a mineral that is essential to healthy blood.

raised from 20 percent to 30 percent by boiling or steaming, after the crop has been washed. Workers then treat the dried figs with potassium sorbate, which prevents mold growth.

Fig Feast

According to some, the finest way to eat figs is in the summer when the fruit is fresh. Sun-warmed, just picked, and fully ripe, figs are tasty served with soft, white cheese and crusty, fresh bread.

And figs are fine eaten dried or in syrup from a can. In India people serve figs, spices, and lime juice in a sugary syrup for a yummy dessert. The French eat poached figs in sauce and simmer figs to accompany roast pork. Figs stuffed with nuts and fig preserves are also prepared in France. People convert figs into paste, syrup, and concentrated flavor powders. Fig nuggets of uniform size are used in candies and cookies.

Great Cookie

These days the Fig Newton is the third most popular cookie in the United States! In 1891 James Henry Mitchell invented the machine that wrapped cookie dough around fig paste. The machine was like a funnel within a funnel. The outer part pushed out a tube of pastry as the inner part pushed out the fig paste to make a long rope of fig-filled treat. At the Kennedy Biscuit Works near Boston, Massachusetts (one of the original bakeries of the Nabisco Group), bakers used the new machinery. They named the cookie after the nearby town of Newton, following their custom of naming treats after towns.

Fig trees can also be grown in greenhouses, where sunlight, temperature, and water are carefully regulated.

Dig In!

Fig Pudding
(12 servings)

2 cups dry, unseasoned
   breadcrumbs
1 cup flour
2 cups ground figs
½ cup sugar
1 teaspoon salt
2 teaspoons baking powder
2 eggs, beaten
1 cup milk, or more as
   needed

The famous figgy pudding from "We Wish You a Merry Christmas" is really a bread pudding with figs. Try making it in the dead of winter when you crave a hearty treat. You can obtain the ground figs by running dried figs through a blender.

   Combine the breadcrumbs, flour, ground figs, sugar, salt, and baking powder. Mix well. Stir in the eggs and enough milk to moisten well. Pour into the top of a double boiler and cover. Steam the mixture for about two hours, keeping one inch of water at a low boil in the bottom of the boiler. Have a tea kettle or a covered pan of hot water ready on the stove, and check the level of the water in the double boiler occasionally. If it falls below an inch, replenish it with boiling water from the kettle. (If you don't have a double boiler, you can improvise by placing a small pan in a larger, water-filled pan.) Serve with a vanilla pudding sauce or with warm cream.

Citrus

Sweet orange [Citrus sinensis]
Lemon [Citrus limon]
Lime[Citrus latifolia]
Grapefruit[Citrus paradisi]
Mandarin[Citrus reticulata]

Among the most enjoyed fruits in the world, citrus is a large family of tropical and subtropical plants. Citrus trees bear glossy, evergreen leaves and have pale blossoms that are remarkably soft and fragrant, attracting honey bees in the morning. The fruit that develops from the blossoms has a sturdy peel that feels like leather. This leathery peel, plus the fruit's fleshy, seedy inside, means that the fruit qualifies as a type of berry called a hesperidium. The spongy outer layer of peel contains the fruit's oils. The peel's white inner layer holds together the fruit sacks (segments), the part of the citrus fruit that people eat.

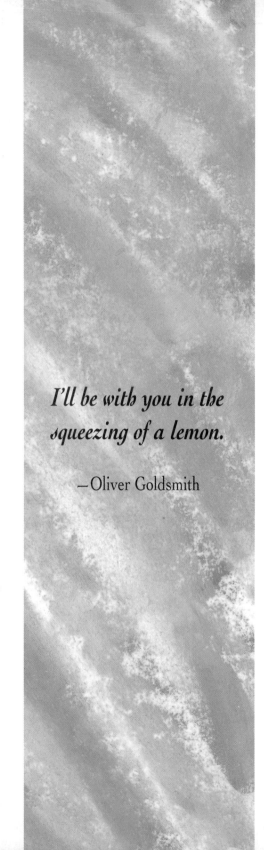

I'll be with you in the squeezing of a lemon.

—Oliver Goldsmith

Prized for its juice and its high vitamin C content, the orange is one of the most popular fruits in the world.

Citrus Origins

The knobby, yellowish citron *(Citrus medica)* may be the parent of all other citrus fruits. Although fruit historians disagree about the citron's precise place of origin, they agree on the fruit's Asian roots. Some historians think that the fruit evolved in India and Myanmar and later moved into China. Others think that the citron came from China and was carried into India.

The sweet orange, *Citrus sinensis,* the world's favorite citrus, began in China as a sour orange, *Citrus aurantium.* The ancient Chinese cultivated the orange by 2500 B.C. Traders from the Chinese mainland may have carried oranges on sea voyages. When fierce weather forced ships to anchor along the southern coast of China and Indochina, sailors heading ashore

Oranges, lemons, limes, and grapefruit are the most familiar members of the large citrus family.

Naga Ranga

Many people believe that the word orange is of Sanskrit (a language of ancient India) origin. A Malaysian legend tells a different tale. Eons ago an elephant came upon a tree bearing golden fruit. He had never seen such a tree and proceeded to eat all its fruit until he burst. Hundreds of years later, a traveler came upon the elephant's skeleton and saw trees with gold fruit growing up from the poor creature's former belly.

Astonished, the traveler exclaimed, "What a fine *naga ranga*." He meant that eating too much of that fruit was a fine way for an elephant to get indigestion. Over time the phrase *naga ranga* evolved into the word orange.

brought oranges with them. The fruit spread along the shore of the South China Sea and the Indian Ocean. Sweet oranges had been bred by the Han Dynasty (202 B.C.–A.D. 220).

The lemon (*Citrus limon*) is a plant species all its own. But some botanists consider it a **hybrid** of unknown ancestors. Others believe that the lemon is the child of the lime and the citron. Even the tree's origins are in doubt. Some think that its origin lies in Italy, while others believe that it is from Asia. In any case, ancient Greeks knew the lemon and wrote about it.

Oranges probably flourished across the Middle East by the time the Greek emperor Alexander the Great died in 323 B.C. Some historians credit Alexander with bringing oranges to the Mediterranean coast.

Roman sea traders brought young orange trees from India to the Roman port of Ostia, probably in the first century. At about the same time, travelers planted orange trees across North Africa. Romans depicted lemons on murals in the 300s and, although they grew lemons at home, they also imported them from their North African colony of Libya. The Moors brought sour oranges and tart lemons to the Iberian Peninsula in the 800s. By the 1200s, orange groves flourished across southern Spain and in parts of Portugal. A Muslim group known as the Saracens brought orange growing to Sicily, the island off the toe of Italy's boot, at about the same time. By 1290 oranges from Spain and Portugal were exported to England.

Arab traders in the 1400s brought sweet oranges across the Middle East. Some

An eighteenth-century French orangery. France's chilly climate forced clever gardeners to grow oranges and other citrus trees indoors.

sources say the sweet orange was grown in Italy and Spain as early as 1450. When Portuguese explorer Vasco da Gama sailed the African and Indian coasts in 1498, he found sweet oranges to sample along the way.

In the centuries to follow, French aristocrats built elaborate greenhouses known as orangeries, which created better environments for the tropic-loving trees. King Louis XIV had an orangery constructed at his palace at Versailles in the 1670s. Sharing space with over three hundred other exotic plants were more than a thousand orange trees planted in silver tubs. The trees were on display for their **ornamental,** perfumed blossoms and to impress the world with the King's wealth. Louis never

It's a Fact!

In 1791 Seminole Indian cooks served William Bartram, a visiting naturalist, steamed red snapper with sliced oranges marinated in honey. Bartram went on to describe local plants and animals in a book called *Travels Through North and South Carolina*.

expected any fruit from his trees. The oranges for the royal menu were imported from Portugal.

Orange over the Ocean

The orange and the lemon first ventured across the Atlantic Ocean in 1493 with Christopher Columbus on his second voyage to the Americas. Columbus carried citrus seeds or seedlings from Spain's mid-Atlantic Canary Islands to the Caribbean island he named Hispaniola (modern-day Haiti and the Dominican Republic). Soon several Caribbean islands were dotted with orange and lemon trees. Portuguese newcomers to South America carried orange seeds in 1499. And in 1516, seedlings reached Panama with the Spaniards.

Two years later the trees were growing in Mexico. Meanwhile, Portuguese settlers planted sweet oranges in their enormous South American colony of Brazil. In 1535 Spanish explorer Francisco Pizarro's men planted oranges, limes, and lemons in Lima, the city they established in Peru. Parrots loved the fruit and carried the seeds with them across the continent.

Spaniards brought oranges to their settlement at St. Augustine, Florida, in 1565, and by 1579 the groves were flourishing. The native people of the area became enthusiastic about oranges, planting them in their own groves and carrying them as food on hunting trips. Pips (seeds) tossed out by traveling orange eaters sprouted into trees that came to mark Indian settlements along the St. John River and eastern shore of Florida.

Catholic priests establishing missions in Arizona and California planted orange trees from Mexican stock throughout the 1700s. The first commercial orange operation wasn't established until 1834, when farmers planted groves near a California village named Los Angeles. Lemon trees also flourished in California.

One popular citrus fruit—the grapefruit—was born on the Caribbean island of Jamaica about 200 years ago. The grapefruit's parent was probably a Malaysian citrus fruit called the pummelo *(Citrus maximus)*. The largest citrus, the pummelo could have mutated into a grapefruit. Or maybe the grapefruit is a hybrid of a pummelo and another plant. The first commercial grapefruit grove was established in Florida around 1890, but it wasn't until after World War II that the fruit's popularity soared. These days it's the second most important citrus fruit worldwide and a

As this Sunkist advertisement from 1917 shows, the orange had become extremely popular with the American public by the early 1900s.

A Bunch of Grapefruit

Ever wonder about the word *grapefruit?* Some people think that the name was given because the fruit on some varieties hangs in bunches, as grapes do. But others give credit to a botanist named John Lunan. In writing about Jamaican plants, he claimed that the large, round, yellow fruit tasted like grapes. Either way, the name *grapefruit* stuck.

key commercial crop in the U.S. states of Texas, Arizona, California, and Florida. By far Florida produces the biggest crop.

Lemons grow well along rain-free coastal areas. Sicily supplies more than 90 percent of the lemons eaten in Italy. Southern France

Naming Names

Oranges come in hundreds of varieties. When you add other citrus, the list gets even longer. Where do these fruits get all their names? Seville, Valencia, and China are only a few of the orange varieties named for places. The Temple orange and Robinson tangerine are named after people. An Italian blood orange, Tarocco, is named for a game played with round cards. Some names, such as Ambersweet (a variety of orange), hint at the taste of the citrus. Other names—for example, the Honeybell—reflect the fruit's shape or appearance. And of course, there is the Ugli fruit—a lumpy-skinned, delicious-tasting combination of a grapefruit, a regular orange, and a sweet tangerine.

and Spain are lemon-growing areas, as are Iran, Israel, Greece, and India. California supplies more than 80 percent of all the lemons used in the United States, but Arizona grows some, too.

My Darling Clementine

The clementine is a favorite North African citrus crop that has become popular with citrus lovers across the globe. The fruit resembles a small, supersweet tangerine, which some experts believe it to be. But many botanists consider the clementine to be the fruit of a union between a sweet orange and a tangerine.

The tangerine and its cousin the satsuma are mandarins (*Citrus reticulata*). These fruits are smaller than a typical orange, although they are usually orange or red in color. The peels are often loose and easy to remove. The fruit sacs may be easy to separate. Mandarin orange trees are resistant to cold, insects, and diseases, which makes them a popular crop.

It's a Fact!

Like the orange and the citron, the lime (*Citrus latifolia*) probably came from India, China, or Malaysia. Most limes sold in the United States are Persian limes.

Citrus trees, such as the orange tree *(left)* and the lemon tree *(below)*, are evergreens with long, shiny leaves and fragrant blossoms. Some orange trees can produce fruit for up to 50 years.

Growing Citrus

Most citrus seedlings are bud grafts. Any citrus rootstock will do. In fact, creative growers can use grafts to create a citrus tree that has one branch of limes, one of lemons, and one of grapefruit.

Planters set the young trees—usually about a year old—in rows 10 or 20 feet apart. Two to five years later, the trees begin to produce fruit. All citrus trees put out light-colored, sweetly scented blossoms. More than six months later, some varieties of citrus fruit might be ready for harvest. Other types need a year and a half to ripen fully. Growers spray the trees with insecticide to keep the trees free of pests. They also work to breed orange, lemon, or tangerine trees that are naturally resistant to diseases.

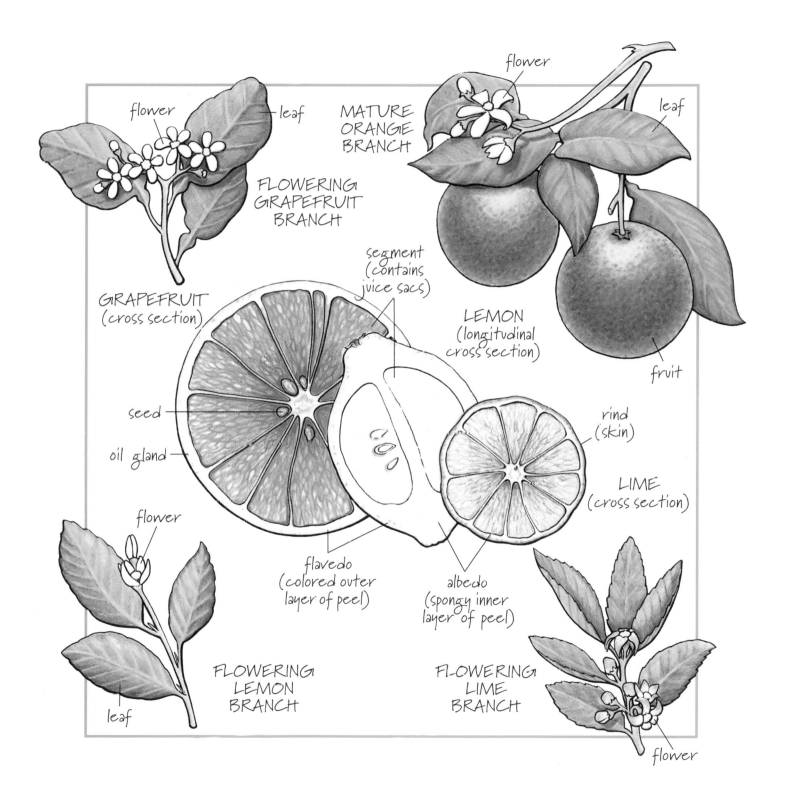

flower

leaf

FLOWERING
GRAPEFRUIT
BRANCH

MATURE
ORANGE
BRANCH

flower

leaf

GRAPEFRUIT
(cross section)

segment
(contains
juice sacs)

LEMON
(longitudinal
cross section)

seed

oil gland

rind
(skin)

fruit

LIME
(cross section)

flower

flavedo
(colored outer
layer of peel)

albedo
(spongy inner
layer of peel)

FLOWERING
LEMON
BRANCH

leaf

FLOWERING
LIME
BRANCH

flower

Citrus Harvest

At orange harvesttime in Florida (early in October), pickers set ladders against the fruit-heavy trees or drive out in cherry-pickers. Workers use clippers to pick the fruit, which they place in canvas bags. The bags can be emptied from the bottom so that the fruit pours into a 900-pound-capacity tub. Periodically a special truck called a goat enters the rows, mechanically picks up the tubs, and dumps them into the truck's hold. When full the goat moves out of the rows and empties its load into a tractor-trailer that can hold up to 45,000 pounds of oranges. Most groves average 7,000 pounds of picked fruit every day of the harvest.

Once the oranges arrive at the packinghouse, the obviously damaged fruit are culled. The grime of the fields is washed off, but so is the thin layer of natural wax that protects the rind. So oranges that will be sold fresh are sprayed with a thin layer of edible wax that protects the skin. Next the clean oranges are graded by electronic sensors or by hand. The oranges are sorted by size. Oranges of uniform size are packed together. Machines or workers carefully pack the graded fruit into boxes or bags, which are shipped to supermarkets.

Picked oranges are placed into large bins that can hold up to 900 pounds of fruit.

Tractor-trailers *(left)* carry oranges directly to a juice-processing plant. When the water is removed, orange juice becomes a syrupy substance known as concentrate *(below)*.

Sip This Citrus!

Oranges to be juiced—often ones that were harvested with a tree shaker—are washed and then pricked. Oil from the pricked peels will later be extracted. Huge extractors release the juice. If the juice is going to be sold fresh, it is pasteurized and bottled. Some juice becomes a frozen concentrate. There is a lot of water in orange juice, so an evaporation device heats the juice to remove that water. What's left—the concentrate—goes into tanks and is chilled to 10 degrees. After it is packaged and sold, people add water to reconstitute the juice.

Orange juice is an important part of breakfast for many North Americans these days. But that wasn't always the case. In 1945 growers on both coasts of the United States were saddled with a surplus of oranges. Determined to sell more oranges, the Sunkist Growers Cooperative of California began promoting the

More than 90 percent of Florida's oranges are processed into juice. The latest trend in juice is labeled "not from concentrate." This means that no water has been added to the product—it's strictly fresh orange juice. In 1998 this product captured 50 percent of the orange juice market for the first time.

slogan Drink an Orange. Of course, it takes several oranges to make one glass of fresh juice. Families began buying orange juicers and drinking fresh orange juice. Canned orange juice was the next innovation, but it didn't taste very good. Fruit scientists scrambled to create the best method of preserving orange juice. In 1948 the Minute Maid company in Florida was first on the market with frozen, concentrated orange

To Your Health!

Oranges have a surprising amount of fiber—more than apples, bananas, broccoli, or potatoes! And oranges have vitamin C, which is essential for people to have healthy tissue. Vitamin C also fights off disease-causing elements called free radicals. The body can't store vitamin C, so people need a dollop every day. Oranges also have folic acid, a B vitamin that helps to prevent brain diseases that can occur in newborns.

To make oranges look uniformly "orange," some are sprayed with a chemical called ethylene to eliminate the green. This orange only got half a spraying.

juice. And in 1954 Florida's Tropicana company developed a way to sell fresh orange juice to markets across the United States.

The thin-skinned, hard-to-peel, and juicy Florida orange hadn't competed well with the California orange as a fresh fruit offering.

The fruit that this farmer holds is a pummelo, the largest of the citrus fruits.

The Washington navel orange—California's favorite—peeled easily, was always completely orange in color (with no green), and its sections broke open easily. But the Florida orange was perfect for juicing.

Three times a week, Tropicana sends a bright orange, mile-long train from Bradenton, Florida, to Jersey City, New Jersey. The refrigerated rail cars carry 1.2 million gallons of juice cooled to 34 degrees. Some juice sloshes in barrels and some in individual containers. It's only a two-day supply for the area's consumers. Consumers in the north-

Mystery Ink

Have you ever wanted to write a secret message? Believe it or not, lemon juice can make it happen! Here's what you need:

Lemon juice
A small dish
A new paintbrush
A piece of paper

Put the lemon juice into the dish. Dip a new paintbrush or your finger into the lemon juice. Use the lemon juice as paint to write a note or paint a picture.

Let the paper dry completely. It looks blank, doesn't it? But hold it in front of a heat source (a toaster, or a hot lightbulb, or even a radiator) for five minutes.

Now what do you see? Let a friend in on the secret, and you can send messages back and forth.

Why does it work? Lemon juice is very acidic. When it hits the paper, it breaks down the paper's starch into sugar. The sugar burns brown at low heat, but the paper isn't affected.

Dig In!

FROTHY ORANGE DRINK (4 SERVINGS)

⅔ cup orange juice concentrate
1 cup water
1 cup milk
1 tsp. powdered milk
½ tsp. vanilla
¼ cup powdered sugar
1 ½ cups ice cubes

Put all of the ingredients in a blender. Blend on high for 2 to 3 minutes, until the ingredients are well blended and frothy.

eastern United States drink 12 gallons of orange juice per person per year, compared to the national average of 5 gallons.

Brazil's Big Business

Brazil is the world's leading producer of oranges, and half of the world's orange juice comes from Brazil. Almost all of the country's production is based in the São Paolo region, where 20,000 farms employ 400,000 workers. They grow China, Valencia, Natal, and Navel oranges, contributing to a billion-dollar juice industry. Most countries that import Brazilian juice mix it with orange

The citron is a sour fruit grown mostly in the Mediterranean area. The peel of the citron is used in candy, but the flesh is rarely eaten.

juice from other places, and then export it to markets across the globe. Brazil leads the world in its high-tech citrus-processing methods.

Eating

Most oranges are eaten fresh or made into juice. But that doesn't mean that they aren't good for cooking, too. In fact, orange ranks as the number-two favorite flavor worldwide. Only chocolate outranks it. Orange wines are favorites in China. Lemon chicken is a tasty main course with Chinese origins. In the Caribbean, islanders enjoy at least two kinds of orange soup— chilled and jellied. Desserts made with oranges are eaten in India. Oranges or lemons flavor a Brazilian black bean dish called *feijoada*. Mexican chicken-lime soup consists of a rich chicken broth into which diners squeeze quartered limes. Lemons add tang to lemon meringue pies, and Key lime pie uses small, tart limes from islands south of Florida.

Sour Seville oranges head to England, where cooks create marmalades. Originally a Portuguese jam made with the skin of quince (an apple relative), modern-day marmalade usually features orange rind instead. To make a tasty spread called curd, cooks mix orange, lemon, or lime juice with sugar, butter, and egg yolks. They cook the mixture until it thickens, let it cool, and

It's a Fact!

Citrus turns up in wine, cosmetics, and even in insect repellent sprays. Citric acid is one of the lemon's significant gifts to industry. First isolated by the Swedish chemist Carl Wilhelm Scheele in 1784, these days citric acid is used as a flavoring and as part of vitamin C tablets. People also use it to clean steel, to preserve color in frozen foods, and as an additive in inks.

then use it to top cakes or other treats. Citrus peel is also made into candy, and it flavors sorbets and ice creams. Citrus extracts are used in a wide range of baked goods. Orange blossoms flavor baked goods and even add flavor to teas.

High Tech

Squeezing all that juice leads to a mound of peels. In Florida the peels, pulp, and seeds are finely chopped in a specially designed machine. The resulting mush is sent through presses that squeeze out any liquid. Finally the mix is run through a dryer. The end product is nutritious cattle feed. The liquid obtained by pressing becomes something called citrus molasses, which can be turned into alcohol. A by-product of that process is an oil used in paint.

Some orange peels are processed differently. They're finely sliced and used to make candy or as ingredients in orange marmalade. The oil from the peel flavors foods and scents perfumes and soaps. Orange seeds are sometimes pressed for their oils, too. The white material that connects the slices is turned into pectin, the component that puts the gluey gel in jelly making.

Glossary

domestication: Taming animals or adapting plants so they can safely live with or be eaten by humans.

ecosystem: A complex community of living and nonliving things that exists as a balanced unit in nature.

graft: To unite two plants by placing a stem or bud of one into a cut in the other, then allowing the two parts to grow together.

hybrid: The offspring of a pair of plants or animals of different varieties, species, or genera.

ornamental: A plant grown for its beauty and not for its food or commercial value.

pesticides: Poisons that growers apply to crops in order to kill unwanted insects or weeds. Pesticides can also harm humans and animals.

photosynthesis: The chemical process by which green plants make energy-producing carbohydrates. The process involves the reaction of sunlight to carbon dioxide, water, and nutrients within plant tissues.

pollination: The placement of pollen on a flower so that fruit will grow from the blossom. Bees pollinate the flowers of many plants.

subtropic: The region near the tropics that shares many characteristics of a tropical climate.

temperate zone: A moderate climate zone that falls either between the Tropic of Cancer and the Arctic Circle in the Northern Hemisphere or between the Tropic of Capricorn and the Antarctic Circle in the Southern Hemisphere.

trellis: A framework of crossed wooden strips used to support climbing plants.

tropics: The hot, wet zone around the earth's equator between the Tropic of Cancer and the Tropic of Capricorn.

Further Reading

Hill, Lee Sullivan. *Farms Feed the World.* Minneapolis: Carolrhoda Books, 1997.

Johnson, Sylvia. *Apple Trees.* Minneapolis: Lerner Publications Company, 1983.

Kite, Patricia L. *Gardening Wizardry for Kids.* Hauppage, NY: Barron's Educational Series, Inc., 1995.

Nottridge, Rhoda. *Vitamins.* Minneapolis: Carolrhoda Books, 1993.

Root, Waverley. *Food.* New York: Simon and Schuster, 1980.

Schneiper, Claudia. *An Apple Tree through the Year.* Minneapolis: Carolrhoda Books, 1986.

Trager, James. *The Food Chronology.* New York: Henry Holt and Company, 1995.

The setting sun lights up the sky over an orange grove in Fresno County, California.

Index

About the Author

Meredith Sayles Hughes has been writing about food since the mid-1970s, when she and her husband, Tom Hughes, founded The Potato Museum in Brussels, Belgium. She has worked on two major exhibitions about food, one for the Smithsonian and one for the National Museum of Science and Technology in Ottawa, Ontario. Author of several articles on food history, Meredith has collaborated with Tom Hughes on a range of food-related programs, lectures, workshops, and teacher-training sessions, as well as *The Great Potato Book*. The Hugheses do exhibits and programs as The FOOD Museum in Albuquerque, New Mexico, where they live with their son, Gulliver.

Acknowledgments

For photographs and artwork: © Steve Brosnahan, p. 5; Tennessee State Museum, detail of a painting by Carlyle Urello, p. 7; AGStock USA: (© Joel Glenn) p. 11, (© Gary Holscher) pp. 17, 21, (© John Marshall) pp. 18 (both), 19, 26, 33, (© Tom Meyers) p. 32, (© Maximilian Stock, Ltd.) pp. 39, 49, (© Randy Vaughn-Dotta) pp. 53, 70, (© Jim Jernigan) p. 61, (© Ed Young) pp. 62, 68 (left), (© Keith Seaman) p. 78; Mary Evans Picture Library, pp. 13, 14, 52, 66; North Wind Picture Archives, pp. 16, 20, 31 (bottom); Photo Researchers, Inc.: (© Hans Reinhard/Okapia) p. 24, (© Jerome Wexler) p. 44, (© Scott Camazine) p. 68 (right), (© Richard T. Nowitz) p. 71 (left), (© Jonathan Wilkins Images) p. 71 (right), (© Alexander Lowry) p. 72; © Walt & Louiseann Pietrowicz/September 8th Stock, pp. 27, 36, 47, 59, 74; Visuals Unlimited: (© Inga Spence) pp. 29, 73, (©Joseph L. Fontenot) pp. 33 (inset), 37, (© E. Webber) p. 34, (© Kjell B. Sandved) p. 54, (© Walt Anderson) p. 56; Art Resource, NY: (© Erich Lessing) p. 30, (Scala) p. 64; Corbis-Bettmann, p. 31; Dinodia Picture Agency: (© Ravi Shekhar) p. 40, (© Vinay Parelkar) p. 43; American Lutheran Church. Used by permission of Augsburg Fortress, p. 41; Steve Foley/Independent Picture Service, p. 45; Corbis/Francis G. Mayer, p. 50; © Gerald Cubitt, p. 57; © Jeff Greenberg, p. 58; © Karlene Schwartz, p. 75. Sidebar and back cover artwork by John Erste. All other artwork by Laura Westlund. Cover Photo by Steve Foley/Independent Picture Service.
For quoted material: p. 4, M. F. K. Fisher, *The Art of Eating* (New York: Macmillan Reference, 1990); p. 10, John Bartlett, *Familiar Quotations*, 13th ed. (Boston: Little Brown, 1955); p. 28, Maryhelen Snyder, "What Cannot Be Pasted in Scrapbooks" (Albuquerque: Watermelon Mountain Press, 1998); p. 38, Jonathon Green, ed., *Consuming Passions* (New York: Ballantine Books, 1985); p. 48, John Bartlett, *Familiar Quotations*, 9th ed. (Boston: Little Brown, 1901); p. 60, Oliver Goldsmith, *She Stoops to Conquer* (New York: Dover, 1991).
For recipes (some slightly adapted for kids): pp. 27, 36, 59, 74, Meredith Sayles Hughes; p. 47, reprinted with permission from *The World in Your Kitchen* by Troth Wells. © 1993. Published by The Crossing Press: Freedom, California.